WHY I HAVE SO MANY CATS

BY LISA J RIVERS

Green Cat Books

Copyright © Green Cat Books 2017

Second Edition
First Edition published 2014

This book is sold subject to the conditions that shall not,
by way of trade or otherwise, be lent, resold, hired out, or
otherwise circulated without the publisher's prior consent
in any form of binding other than that in which it is
published and without a similar condition Including this
condition being imposed on the subsequent purchaser

Green Cat Books

www.green-cat.co/books

To Emma,

meow!

Lisa
xo.

Contents

1. Why I have so many cats pt1
2. Kitty
3. Simba
4. Tigger
5. Beppe
6. Raven
7. Starfire
8. Tom
9. Willow
10. Tinkerbell
11. Binx
12. Tigerlily
13. Felix
14. Ninja
15. Marley
16. Olly
17. Eric
18. Rosie
19. Misty
20. Kenny
21. Clementine
22. Why I have so many cats pt2

WHY I HAVE SO MANY CATS

pt1

I have an obsession with cats

Many people claim

Yes I'm THE mad cat lady

That is my claim to fame.

I really couldn't care less

What other people think

Some people smoke or do drugs

Some others love to drink.

My love is my fur babies

I admit that from the start

My cats are my alcohol, My drug,

They're in my heart.

So there's no need to criticise

We all have a passion

We have addictive natures

Cars, football, rugby, fashion.

My passion is the kitties

I care for them so much.

They've been in my life for many years

And that is that, as such

Don't judge me for my quirkiness

Indeed, I may be mad

Read my poems and then decide

It can't really be so bad

KITTY

My best friend bought me my first cat

Sleek and black, her name was Kitty

Oh my she was just a baby

So beautiful, she was so pretty

She proudly took pride of place

Just us 3 girls in our house

Me, my toddler and the cat

Who brought us love, and the occasional mouse

It turned out she was epileptic

When one day I had a scare

She had a fit in front of me

Then she peed in my new chair

I took her to the vet next day

But nothing could be done for her

We would just have to put up with it

Which really was a bummer

She coped quite well, had a lovely life

She even had a litter

Then got run over on the main road

That really was a shitter

SIMBA

Simba was a ginger kitten

Looked like a mini Lion King

(I'd never even seen the film)

But the name just seemed to suit him

He'd stalk the giant dog we had

And play all day and night

They really were the best of pals

It was such a funny sight

It turned out daddy didn't like him

He really was a prat

Apparently he was a "dog man"

"Get rid of that bloody cat!"

Poor Simba, he just had to go

"It's me or that damn moggy"

In hindsight I should have chosen Simba

But chose him and the doggy

What a stupid choice I made

Of that I became aware

When he left us with that "damn dog"

And instead had an affair

So there I was left all alone

Well me, the dog and child

A full time job, a childminder

And a dog that was kind of wild

It was just too much, I could not cope

And Dick didn't seem to care

Poor Zak (the dog),he was too big

In a little house it wasn't fair

I asked the dog's home to take him back

We'd adopted him you see

They understood the need for this

But it was not easy

I'm not as heartless as I sound

It was the best for Zak

And low and behold, a few months later

Dick he did come back

He hardly noticed his dog had gone

He didn't give a toss

And continued having his affairs

Then left, which was not a loss!

He came and left for several women

And I always seemed to be in tears

Eventually I had enough

I'd wasted several years

I should have kept the bloody cat

And saved myself the heartache

I moved away and took the kid

Like a scene from a prison break

I'd secretly got myself a place

Away from him, the Dick

It all happened in a blur

It really was so quick

I digress from my love of cats

Eventually I got Tigger

He was a gorgeous tabby cat

And my love of cats got bigger

TIGGER

Tigger was the biggest cat

That I have ever had

He didn't spend much time at home

He was an outdoor lad

BEPPE

Along came Beppe, a tiny chap

Black and white, as I recall

He got on really well with Tigger

They really had a ball

Tigger wandered off one day

As he often did

But this time he didn't return

Left Beppe alone, poor kid

A few weeks later something odd

Was happening round here

Beppe was clearly not a boy

When babies did appear!

Badger, Tigs and Patch

Were miracles indeed!

They looked just like their daddy

Who had ran off with such speed

Tigger didn't want the job

He wouldn't be the last

Many daddies did the same

Although others weren't so fast

So Beppe was a single mum

Alone with her young litter

Luckily cats cope quite well

And their feelings don't get bitter

RAVEN

The first time I saw Raven

I had a choice of two

She lay all snuggled with her twin

I didn't have a clue

How could I choose between the two?

It really wasn't easy

I simply had to have them both

My smile was so cheesy

That is when I became

The mad cat lady, dizzy!

I took them home to show the kids

It really was quite busy

Raven was quite confident

She strolled right out the carrier

Her sister wasn't quite so keen

She hid behind a barrier

We cooed and coaxed but there she stayed

Until we dragged her out

She ran away and hid from us

We didn't even shout

But this poem is about her sister

I should stay on track.

Raven was so gorgeous,

Ginger, brown and black.

She took the role of cat in charge

And still nothing has changed

Nine years on she's still the boss,

A little more deranged!

All the others have respect

They bow their heads in fear

She'll walk past them all regally

They stay until it's clear

She acts like she should be the queen

She does deserve a crown

She wouldn't even stand for that

She only wears a frown

But despite that frosty front

She really is a dear

She loves to have her belly rubbed

But growls if you go near

She has to give permission first

She'll lie down for a stroke

Approach her with such caution

You don't want your hand broke!

She isn't really nasty

Just choosy of her friends

And if she really likes you

That friendship never ends

STARFIRE

Starfire is Raven's kid sister

More a princess than a queen

When she first arrived at home

She wasn't really keen

Learning from the previous

Mistakes that I had made

I quickly nipped them down the vets

And made sure they were spayed

That Christmas was a special one

We bought a brand new tree

The kittens liked to climb in it

It was a sight to see

Something startled Starfire

One day, perhaps the lights?

She leapt out of the Christmas tree

And gave us all a fright

Tangled up in loads of tinsel

She scarpered round the room

Dragging half the Christmas tree

We thought that she was doomed

We tried to chase her to set her free

But boy! she was so fast

We ducked and dived away from harm

We knew it couldn't last

Eventually we got a grip

And grabbed her safe and sound

We reassured her all was fine

The tinsel was unwound

This hadn't really helped her nerves

It had just made her jumpy

We will never forget that day

Starfire, you're a numpty!

TOM

"I know 2 cats that need a home

Their mummy doesn't want them"

That was like a call from heaven

"I'll be right over in ten..."

Tom was such a darling boy

Cute and fluffy and black

His sister was too poorly

So we would have to come back

Willow followed shortly after

As soon as she was healthy

Now we had a house of cats

Our lives felt rich and wealthy

Tom and Willow settled nicely

Despite the wrath of Raven

Tom was quite an outdoor cat

Which lead to his path to heaven

We lost poor Tom

at 5 months old

Oh no, what had that car done?

We wrapped him in a pillowcase

A now he's in the garden

We all had many tears that night

It wasn't very good

To lose poor Tom at such an age

But then adopted Bud

WILLOW

Willow is our quiet girl

Her meow is quite silent

She's a very loving cat

But with Marley can be violent

Marley really winds her up

Follows here everywhere

Looks at her adoringly

But Willow, she does stare

Back to when we first got her

You know, when she was better?

When we were busy mourning Tom

She went and had a litter!

Five black fluff balls, all the same

We hadn't had a clue

she started getting fat

And let out a massive MEW

Sat down on the comfy sofa

She snuggled on my lap

And gave birth on my duvet cover

That was the end of that!

KITTENS! KITTENS! EVERYWHERE!

How many did we have?

We tried to keep them in a box

Ha ha ha that was daft!

Surely this could get no worse

Although we loved them dearly

We could not feed that many mouths

We had to sell them, clearly

We found a lovely home for two

It was quite far away

I drove them to meet their new humans

Much to my dismay

The journey that was quite chaotic

They both wanted to escape

The box balanced on the front seat

They ate through the sticky tape

Climbing out to take a look

I had to stop the car

I had a little chat with them

"Come on, it's not too far!"

Eventually I got them there

It was love at first sight

They loved them loads and wanted more

So I drove back there that night

Two more kittens, identical

Went to their new home

The humans were so overjoyed

Just left, their brother, on his own

Binx, we named him, he was cute

Just like his mum and Uncle Tom

His story we will get to soon

It won't be very long

TINKERBELL

Tinkerbell was five months old

And her dad had called her Bud

She always seemed to be kept outside

Even though she was really good

I took her home and showed the kids

They squealed with delight

She was my very first cat that sat on my lap

And was very very light

One day she started acting weird

Like she had broke her back

I took her to the vet next day

"She's on heat, so please don't slack"

"Don't let her out the house right now

I know that will be tough"

I told the kids, they got excited

And soon she was up the duff

They sneakily had let her out

They wanted bundles of fur

We didn't know Willow was pregnant

The kids, they didn't care

Shortly after Willow's litter

Tinkerbell followed suit

Gave birth behind the sofa

Out the four babies did shoot

She left the first one, a girl, and wandered off

To have the 3 cute boys

The girl needed resuscitating

It was tense, we were all poised

Would the baby girl survive?

It was very scary

But Tigerlily took a breath

And things didn't seem so hairy

She became a tough little girl
But looked as cute as a daisy
We pampered her all the time
She really was quite lazy

The boys were cute as well, of course
But we couldn't keep them all
Sox and Thomas had a new home
Tigerlily was "too cute and small"

We kept her coz we'd formed a bond
The kids managed to convince me
Oh and let's not forget
Felix As he was "simply dreamy"
The kids were clearly running rings
And ganging up to keep them
How many cats in the house now?
2? 4? 6? 8? 10?

BINX

Black cats are meant to be good luck

But not this poor little might

We don't know what happened to him

He disappeared one night

TIGERLILY

Tigerlily, the survivor

Was a tiny little thing

Verging on the feral side

All creatures she did bring

Dragging massive birds around

Still flapping in her mouth

She'd chase them round the garden

And down the garden path

Maybe just a bit too feral

She'd disappear for days

Then turn up again like nothing's wrong

It was one of her ways

One day she didn't return home

A familiar thing for us

But one day we were moving home

And were in a terrible rush

We waited and shouted out for her

With the others in the car

We searched and hunted everywhere

We'd hoped she wasn't far

We were moving many miles away

So couldn't just come back

We knew we wouldn't find our Lily

We had to face the fact

Disappointedly we left

Reluctant as we would miss her

We hope she's ok with her new life

And receiving lots of care

FELIX

Felix is our chunky boy

Black and white just like the advert

My eldest loved him instantly

Surely keeping him wouldn't hurt?

Seven years we've had him now

He is our pride and joy

Been family since the day he was born

And our special, big fat boy

He meows really loud when he wakes up

It's like he's shouting with a yawn

He's first in line for tuna scraps

But not so keen on prawns

He likes to make his presence known

And is very affectionate

He crushes you when he's on your lap

A lumpy, bumpy cat

NINJA

Tigerlily was her name

But we weren't having that

There was only ever one Tigerlily

We had to rename this cat

She came from our new neighbour's house

They couldn't cope with her

We thought of so many names

But why did we call her Ninja?

Cookie, Fudge and Fluffy

Were the names leading the race

Until she climbed up my bedroom curtain

And threw herself at my face!

She'd scale the window, wardrobes too

And jump and lunge at me

And hang from the curtain rails at times

It was a sight to see

One day we couldn't find her

Oh no! Not this again!

What was that loud banging sound?

We searched around in vain

Eventually we found her

In the tumble dryer!

Been switched on just a mili-second

That made me perspire!

She was ok, thank goodness

A little dizzy maybe

She calmed down just after that

And wasn't quite so crazy

Marley is the tiniest

She is obsessed with Willow

She follows her round everywhere

But then sleeps on my pillow

Maybe she's a mummy's girl

She likes to snuggle tight

Or maybe it's coz Willow

Sleeps next to me at night!

She has a funny nickname

We sometimes call her Marmite

Coz when she farts it smells quite pungent

It gives us quite a fright

She's mummy to the other cats

I'm yet to mention here

You'd think we'd learn our lesson

But we love our cats so dear

Felix was "done" years ago

But has adopted the kits'

The house is full of harmony

They love their Daddy Felix

He kisses them and licks their heads

But Marley doesn't like them

She hisses, spits and slaps them all

Even baby Clem

OLLY

Olly is the oldest one

Of all of Marley's brood

He's chunky like his step-daddy

He really loves his food

Identical to brother Eric

It's hard to tell them apart

Olly has a white patch on his nose

While Eric is a tart

Olly couldn't give a damn

He is a bit aloof

But Eric flirts with everyone

Quite clingy, that's the truth

Olly doesn't need attention

He's happy left alone

When he's in a bad mood

He walks around and roams

One winter he went a wandering

We didn't see him for days

Oh no! Not this again, can't cope

My brain went in a daze

But one day he wandered back

Christmas Day it was

He didn't understand the fuss

It was the bestest Christmas!

ERIC

Eric has a drippy nose

He flings snot everywhere

It drips when he kisses me

It's just too much to bear

He waits for opportunities

To sit down on your lap

It doesn't matter if you're not comfy

He needs to have his nap

He nudges you to have a kiss

And meows if you don't listen

There's no way to avoid that kiss

And the drippy nose that glistens

ROSIE

Gorgeous Rosie was their sister

Another sorry tale

Yes she did go missing too

We searched but we did fail

A few days later she reappeared

But not quite as we hoped

Laid gently by the garden gate

I don't know how we coped

We hugged and kissed her gently

We knew we were too late

The neighbour said he'd found her

And put her by the gate

Is it best to know this fate

Or is ignorance just bliss?

At least we know the outcome

And could give her one last kiss

MISTY

Misty was so gobby

Since the day that she arrived

She meowed at us so loudly

To let us know she was alive

We nicknamed her Gabby

Til her new mummy gave her a new name

Now she's known as Misty

And on Facebook she has fame

Her new mummy loves her very much

And posts pics of her online

I'm regularly tagged in the pics

She's lovely and divine

She's a pampered princess

And very safe and sound

It's nice to stay in touch with her

As her Nannie I am proud

KENNY

When Kenny and Clementine were born

They looked identical

The same scenario as before

We were going to have a ball

We noticed Kenny had a smudge

On his nose and bum

And Clementine, a white patch

Like she had a nappy on

So Kenny we named Smudge

And Clem; Baby was her name

It stayed like that for a short while

Until the kids played a video game

Kenny and Clementine were characters

"Our favourites" they did insist

And changed their names immediately

Despite that I was pissed!

I didn't want to change their names

It didn't seem that fair

They were used to the names we'd given them

Not that the kids did care

Kenny is adventurous

He likes to climb our legs

And when it's feeding time at home

He smiles, meows and begs

He sits down on our shoulder

And likes to watch us eat

He tries to grab the food we have

And won't admit defeat

CLEMENTINE

Clementine, our Baby

A tiny, fluffy thing

Nowhere near as innocent

As her cute looks seem to bring

She opens the refrigerator

And tries to steal the meats

The others sit and watch her

Then nick some, what cheats!

She doesn't stand for nonsense

She's as a strong as any male

And when she fights or gets scared

She fluffs up her big tail

She likes to cuddle armpits

It really makes her purr

But when she's bored she gets up and goes

And leaves us smothered in fur

WHY I HAVE SO MANY CATS

Pt 2

Why do I have so many cats?

People often ask

Feeding, litter trays and flea meds

It really is a task

But full of bitter sweet moments

I really have to say

Why shouldn't I have so many cats?

I don't regret a day

From falling off the window sill

And landing on my head

To rolling over next to me

And falling off my bed

Snorting, hissing, growling

Kissing, snuggles too

These non cat lovers wouldn't know

They didn't have a clue

They've given me so much love

Every day is full of joys

They're better than any man I've had

I love my girls and boys!

COMING SOON....

WINDING DOWN

DEBUT NOVEL

BY LISA J RIVERS

JUNE 2017

ALSO AVAILABLE WITH GREEN CAT BOOKS

LIFE WELL LIVED
LUNA FELIS

"Preparing for death is one of the most empowering things you can do. Thinking about death clarifies your life."
Candy Chang

There are two things that are guaranteed - birth and death. Few of us are ready for the latter, but sometimes putting things into order can put our minds at rest. Things we wish we had said to someone, but never had the time or courage.

Luna has designed this book like a scrapbook, for the owner to complete in their own time, focusing on what they would like in the event of their passing. Last wishes, memories and important information are sections included within the book.

"This Book is excellent, just what I needed! Many Thanks!"

ARE YOU A WRITER?

We are looking for writers to send in their manuscripts.

If you would like to submit your work, please send to

books@green-cat.co

Green Cat Books

Made in the USA
Middletown, DE
29 May 2017